The God in Me Will Emerge: Poems

**THE GOD IN ME WILL EMERGE:
POEMS**

by

Andrew Buckner

The God in Me Will Emerge: Poems Copyright © 2024 Andrew Buckner

Published by Requiem Press.

All rights reserved. No part of this publication may be reproduced or transmitted in any form or by any means, electronic or mechanical, including photocopy, recording, or any information storage and retrieval system, without permission in writing from the publisher.

https://requiempress.weebly.com/
https://awordofdreams.com/

Cover image Vecteezy.com & Pixabay.com

A Requiem Press Book

ISBN: 979-8-9899561-7-3

ACKNOWLEDGMENTS

The following collection of verse is dedicated, as always, to my wife, Valerie, my daughters, Bianca and Arianna, and to my mother, Pamela, whose kind words, love, and support keep the pen moving on the page.

Further acknowledgments go out to the following publications which originally published some of the poetry found in this volume. They are Sontag Mag, which published "The Body is a Glorified Hotel" in their debut issue, Without Borders, in January, 2024, Resurrection Mag, which published "I'm Being Crucified" in their second volume, Crucify, on March 31st, 2024, Genrepunk Magazine, which published "A Gust (Aghast): The Horror of Finding Creation in the Commonplace" on their website on August 21st, 2024, Spare Parts Lit, which published "A Weary Traveler on the Byways of Invention (An Open Letter to AI Writing Tools)" in their second issue of ART/ificial on January 31st, 2024, Midsummer Dream House, which published "'Such is Life,' the Slithering Centuries Whisper" on January 30th, 2024 on their website, Stanza Cannon, which published "In the Mental Moors is Where I Found You" and "A Philosophy of Memory" in both audio and text form in their eighth issue on January 20th, 2024, Poverty House, which published "Cemetery Mother" on December 13th, 2023 on their website, Naked Cat Publishing, which published "Like Kurt Cobain in a High School Gymnasium" in their 90's Pop and Grunge: Grime issue, Glass: A Journal of Arts, which published the experimental poems "A Uniform, 'One Size Fits All Populace" and "And I Have No Story to Tell…" on their website, Shadow Pond Journal, which published "Untitled Haiku #2" in their Winter 2023 issue on December 11th, 2023, Persephone's Fruit, which published "A Mirrored Projection" on their website in 2024, Papers Publishing, which published "A Life Passed, A Life in Need" on pages 38-39 of their second issue, Sit With Me, and Lothlorien Poetry Journal who published the poems "All of Earth is a Church and No One Wants My Religion", "The Screech on the Crank of Progress", "The Snarling Brute, the Bloodthirsty Creature at My Door", and "In a Stolen Vehicle of Insight " on their website on March 13th, 2024. The opener, "Everything is Not Meant to be Understood", was published by Sinkhole Magazine in 2024. "Howl of the Crazed Eye Fish Monster Bathing in Oceans of Blood" was previously published by Red String Magazine in their debut issue in 2024. The title poem, "The God in Me Will Emerge", was initially published in Issue #65 of Alien Buddha Press, which was published in August, 2024!

Page	CONTENTS
1	EVERYTHING IS NOT MEANT TO BE UNDERSTOOD
2	THE CREATURE OF MY OWN DESTRUCTION
5	THE GHASTLINESS OF MY OWN VISAGE, THE UNFETTERED MIND
7	THE BODY IS A GLORIFIED HOTEL
9	PECKED TO DEATH BY VULTURES IN A FIELD
10	IN THE MENTAL MOORS IS WHERE I FOUND YOU
11	I'M FALLING INTO MEDIOCRITY QUITE NICELY
12	EXPERI/MENTAL, OR A SWIMMING, PARASITIC CIRCLE
14	THE WORD "VISIONARY" IS OVERUSED
16	THE GOD IN ME WILL EMERGE
17	I'M BEING CRUCIFIED
20	ALL OF EARTH IS A CHURCH AND NO ONE WANTS MY RELIGION
22	THE GOD OF EVERYTHING AND NOTHING, THE LANDLORD OF THE DEAD
24	UNTITLED HAIKU #1
25	DEAR DIVINE FORMS, I BEG OF THEE TO SIMPLY, SINCERELY TYPE "THE END"
27	WE NEED TO REBEL AS WILDLY, CHAOTICALLY AS WE POSSIBLY CAN
29	A TEACHER PREACHING SUMMERTIME IN THE EVER-FRUITFUL GARDEN OF THE SENSIBILITIES
32	A LIFE PASSED, A LIFE IN NEED
34	THE BEAUTIFUL PAIN OF A VOW TAKING FLIGHT

35	LIKE CONCRETE, A STRANGE HABIT FORMED
36	A SMILE NIBBLING STILL
37	A CHILD-LIKE TASTE OF SUN, LIGHT
38	THE SUM OF A LIFE: A ONE-SCENE PLAY
40	A FALSE GLIMMER TO THE NOSTALGIC MIND
41	I, LITERARY EXPLORER, FOUND VOICE, SELF
42	A MIRRORED PROJECTION
43	LET ME DRINK OF YOUR NECTAR, SWEET SPRING!
44	THE BEAUTIFUL BEASTS BEFORE THEM
45	UNTITLED HAIKU #2
46	THE ONCE IN-DEPTH WORLD OF OUR WORDS
47	A GUST (AGHAST): THE HORROR OF FINDING CREATION IN THE COMMONPLACE
48	LIFE, FRESHLY FALLEN
49	HOWL OF THE CRAZED EYE FISH MONSTER BATHING IN OCEANS OF BLOOD
50	A LIFE TAKES HOLD. OR THE WOLF MAN (2024)
52	THE POTENTIAL, IMPENDING EMPTINESS (OF THE HEAD)
53	GLASS CORRIDORS
54	"SUCH IS LIFE," THE SLITHERING CENTURIES WHISPER
56	THE MOST INTIMATE FORM OF GOSSIP
58	A WEARY TRAVELER ON THE BYWAYS OF INVENTION (AN OPEN LETTER TO AI WRITING TOOLS)
60	THE PAINTING LIED
61	A BRIEF CONTEMPLATION OF A LONG LIFE

62	CEMETERY MOTHER
63	IN A STOLEN VEHICLE OF INSIGHT
66	A UNIFORM, "ONE SIZE FITS ALL" POPULACE
68	(AND I HAVE NO STORY TO TELL AND I HAVE NO STORY TO TELL AND I HAVE NO)
70	MY VAMPIRE SELF HAS HIS DAY
73	I NOW UNDERSTAND THE DEEPLY ENTRENCHED PHILOSOPHICAL UNDERPINNINGS OF WHY OTHER PEOPLE SHOWING UP AT A MOVIE I AM ATTENDING BOTHERS ME SO MUCH
74	LIKE KURT COBAIN IN A HIGH SCHOOL GYMNASIUM
77	THE UNUSUALLY TALKATIVE, PROFANITY-LIPPED VERSION OF ME
79	THESE HIGH-TECH 1950's B-MOVIE EFFECTS
81	FIRE IN THE CRUMBLING CAVES OF A MELODIC PLANET
82	THE BIRD HAS FALLEN FROM THE SKY
83	A MERE FLOWER– THE ENTIRE SPECTRUM OF HUMAN EMOTION
84	SILENT PEASANT SPIRALING DOWNWARD, NOVEMBER TREE
86	GRETA THE MINEX AND THE UNIVERSAL MAGICIAN
87	UNTITLED HAIKU #3
88	POEM WHERE I CONTEMPLATE THE END OF THE WORLD
89	A PHILOSOPHY OF MEMORY
90	THE SCREECH ON THE CRANK OF PROGRESS
92	THE TALE CLIMAXES IN AN UNEXPECTEDLY OPTIMISTIC WAY
93	ABOUT THE AUTHOR

EVERYTHING IS NOT MEANT TO BE UNDERSTOOD

A shovel, an impulse, a hot burning in the back of the head, and a hole opening up as I find the chairs I lost to the unusually temperate early February weather. The lawn opens up evermore, as if it were a gazebo in mid-summer, and I taste the 9 a.m. coffee, mentally peruse the novels, poetic tomes, and collective essays that I enjoyed in this light blue bit of plastic over the decade it has been in and a part of my life with a newfound burst of appreciation.

The hole cracks open more. An ant crawls out and tells me that even he, too, gets tired of the load he has to carry on his back for his colony, his nest, his army before the crater shrinks in on itself, the earth nearly pulls me in, and an owl perches on my shoulder. He tells me that he, too, is not of the night. This is regardless of what those with similar beaks, eyes, and feathers tell him.

"Man is a model of nature. Man is not of nature. All are different branches from different trees. All are branches of the same tree."

The autumn leaves tell me they want to fall skyward, yet gravity keeps commanding them to come down, to drown in, and fall before the great goddess of the winter snow, to be exactly like all of the other popping colors that they bloomed with and, in turn, catapulted to their doom alongside like bloodstained brothers, soldiers in an environmental war.

"Is this a whisper or a truth that I, a mere extension of man, a mere extension of nature, was always busying myself too much with to hear? What will we do with this knowledge? Does this knowledge matter? Who am I to ask?"

I am knowledge, an extension of the tree from which it derives, yet I know nothing.

The hole widens. So does my heart, my mind, and I find myself sitting on the chair I thought I lost, reading, contemplating, ignoring the voices that dictate what I must do at all times and listening to the internal voice within, and a tiny vine, a branch of wisdom and understanding, sprouts from my world-weary palms.

"Maybe not everything is meant to be understood," a voice starts.

THE CREATURE OF MY OWN DESTRUCTION

I.

Eternity's harbor
Lags behind
The creature of my own destruction—
The black and white,
Indestructible
Fiend I've chased
Through a concrete village
Where mental graffiti sprawls
And sticks to the fingertips
Of the seamstress, loner, sole dweller
Of said village, Ambition,
As the herculean wreckage
From the behemoth, Thy Past,
Thy Recurring Failures,
Who taunts the seamstress
Into selling his only property, Time,
Into believing the lies that a little
More effort, a little more productivity
Will make his immaterial name
Immemorial,
Into looking past the dead fish,
Weeping eyes, children of continued
Invention who endure as orphaned
Because one soul, one idea
Was more pressing in that penultimate
Moment of decision than
The now wandering youth
Who stalks the cracked roads of said village
Searching, seeking for parents
Who will accept him,
Who will clothe him,
Who will nurture him,
Who will put shoes on his
Broken and bloody feet
While he wanders amid

His wartorn surroundings
Noting the song of the wind
As it whips around his bruised flesh,
His wounded side, his aching head
Spilling with thoughts,
Shrill with vultures,
Shoulder-sitting devils,
Incantations of his own self,
His own mind
That cackle, "What will you do
With your life now?
It's taken you forty years of effort,
Forty years of creation
To even convince yourself
You have the capability
To write worthwhile tomes
That audiences will tolerate,
Let alone applaud,
To feel as if you are finally ready
To begin
Your long in-process
Literary journey–
And no one knows your name!
Your work won't endure!
You're a beggar, a peasant!
Just accept your fate!
All you had is this village you created
And now it is nil–
An archaic instrument–rusty, decrepit,
Imploding with time."

II.

"Dream with me," she says
And, stone-eyed, I rouse from my slumber–
An abandoned villager, now a ready passenger
Toggling between the reality I exist in
And the reality I want to escape from–

A
time
traveler,
A
Child,
An
Artist

Beaten,
Broken,
But
Again

Inspired.

THE GHASTLINESS OF MY OWN VISAGE, THE UNFETTERED MIND

                      I fear the ghastliness of my own visage,
                      The unfettered mind

Like the social media echo chamber   Returning to blind eyes, deaf ears
Only the snot-nosed monster   Of their own ideals
        Brutality packaged as
Delicacy   Luminosity   Artistry

When it's all ugly   Dog shit run over by a lawn mower
        By a kid who only
Wants paid for his work   And didn't check his gas or oil before
                        Robotically enacting his daily chore

                      And dreams, like we all do,   Of
            better times
Of putting the sleeping mask on through his days   And not seeing
The curtains pulled, which bend backwards the morning light
                            From the horrors of the outside world
                            From the creatures of the modern day

The beasts with fangs and claws and endless wallets at his door

The generic beauty   Artificial allure
                            Trap we've all broken our necks and backs
                            Trying to adhere to
                            When time heartily chuckles at our actions
                            And, holding his hefty gut, simply spits out, "Nah, son!"

Is why I am proud of the way the curtains bend the morning light

Because I fear that what I might see
Is some of me in the snarling brute, the bloodthirsty creature at the door–

           The ghastliness of my own visage,
                The unfettered mind.

THE BODY IS A GLORIFIED HOTEL

The body is a glorified hotel—
A mass of straining, struggling,
Yet stalwart muscle,
Connected epidermal islands,
Fiery planets of unexplored sensations,
A confounding, often confused internal cosmos
Guided by the searing stars of instinct, faith,
Hope, fear, and imagination—
We are forced to facilitate, vacate
By the all-seeing, almighty
God of expectation, time

By society's forced worship
At the bloodstained altar of material gain,
It's hivelike mentality,
It's machinelike ability
To make us forever stand in service,
Warehousemen at the assembly line,
Of producing the same bland, generic,
Culturally acceptable product
For as long as this hotel
Is in our name.

The body is a glorified hotel—
Roof slumping, insecure, shaking
By the gale force winds
Of the irritated, swollen sting,
The punching fist of judgment
Towards the curve of the mouth,
The gleam in the eyes,
The hue of the skin,
The gender, abilities
Of the singular building,
Our body, our flesh,
In which we are sole inhabitant,
The singular palace in which we are born.

Though the walls are frequently claustrophobic, confining
And the constant familiarity of our own company
Is simultaneously too much and too little,
Too routine and too alien,
This glorified hotel, our body, our flesh,
Is our shelter, perfect imperfections and all,
For which we are custodian, defender, builder,
Occupant, owner, manager,
The beacon, the light keeper, all.

We are the carpenter, architect,
The interior blueprint designs are uniquely,
Beautifully our own,
In this body, glorified hotel
Planted proudly in the soil of self:

A glorious, gaudy construction
That we should be able to
Freely decorate, illuminate,
Facilitate, commemorate—

A glorious, gaudy construction
Which we should be happy
To liberate, dwell

Past the ever-darkening eclipse,
The horizons of sight, sound,
The physical plane,
Into the aftermath of memory,
The aftermath of grit, grain, pain—
The aftermath of now.

PECKED TO DEATH BY VULTURES IN A FIELD

I laugh, almost painfully now, at my youthful fear:
Being abducted at night by aliens.
Now, as something of a budding adult at forty years,
What causes insomnia, a rippling of ruddy guts twisting within

Is something, anything bad happening to my two beautiful children,
Failing at being a husband, that these bullet-like words dutifully cast to the page
Like time out the window, ashes from fingertips, an unfelt wind
Will never be witnessed, an electronic comet will wipe them out in a rage,

The insipid question will linger from the lips of elders once again,
"Do you still write?"
And no one will even ask a follow-up inquiry when
I say I have a book that was just accepted for publication, as if the light

I try frantically, with ever-reaching but stubborn fingertips, to wield
Is too harsh, obscure, insignificant for their superior sights
So, like the scarecrow, all my creative output, worth, inner-plight
Must be abandoned, ignored,
Left to be pecked to death by vultures in a field.

IN THE MENTAL MOORS IS WHERE I FOUND YOU

In the mental moors is where I found you,
A mass of motionless muscle among the weeds,
Calling out to the shores
To come home, long past curfew
With only the vascular night skies to lead

The deteriorating vessels of past, future mingling
Confused by the specter-laden fog;
A deathless war,
The body taken by the mind's greed—
Skeletons put their key in the door

Of memory formation, loss;
The endless ballet
For which we are all dancers for a day

And as the fingers clasp their weighty dust
We all fade away.

I'M FALLING INTO MEDIOCRITY QUITE NICELY

I'm falling into mediocrity quite nicely—

Merry bursts of laughter deceive
The tightness encasing the chest
Worry wears masks of hope, relieved
Through dangerous glares, class arrest.

I'm falling into mediocrity quite nicely.

Or, so self echoes
As party speech, the surface continues to be glorified
("The pool here is quite shallow")
I toil, toil, toil while thy own appearance is vilified.

I'm falling into mediocrity quite nicely.

Ignored, the cold shoulder given by all who encounter me,
A product of my obvious indifference to material things,
Still the thorns on the rose of vanity
Summon a ruddy bloom. It still stings.

I'm falling into mediocrity quite nicely.

And the pleasantly-worded rejections are ice dressed in a coat, tie—
A long-expected punch in the gut—
So, I hide my hideous hair, aging eye
Inside a "Let's just stare at the floor" strut.

I'm falling into mediocrity quite nicely.

As I tire of the rising tide of anticipation encapsulating,
Drowning me to leave a familiar emptiness, hollow shell
The crowd gathers to laugh and sing
Dante's latest iteration of hell.

I'm falling into mediocrity quite nicely

EXPERI/MENTAL, OR A SWIMMING, PARASITIC CIRCLE

A swimming, parasitic circle,
We drink Crutch-A because Crutch-B
Makes us think of Crutch-A etc.,
Forms in never-idle hand motions,
Lifting to lips, parting like legs
Eagerly accepting, rejecting,
Slapping against the recently wiped, peanut-strewn
Mahogany of a rain slick barroom table.

A swimming, parasitic circle,
The endless excuses to leave the home–
A movie, a Dollar Store run calls—
Echoing ghostly pangs of loneliness
As the monster of emptiness
Born from boredom, an endless
Pressure to do something, be something
"To live", "To experience life
While breath still pulsates through my lungs"
Suffocates with the invisible extremities
Of limitless possibilities—

An angry customer
Which must be serviced exactly as he demands
Every moment of every day—

A swimming, parasitic circle,
Forcing art upon the eyes, the ears
And trying desperately, feebly–
A snail pushing upwards against the rushing tide,
A snail pushing upwards against the avalanche, snow–
To create something entirely new,
Or, even, something slightly different–
Fingers frantically typing "Experi/MENTAL"
When simply penning "Experimental"
Would suffice–
Crawls in my greasy brain, my scalp, my hair
Like bugs slithering,

Trying desperately to find a home
Like the legions of my own identical thoughts
Festering to and fro from holes, corners, floorboards,
Like the crutches we use to get from Point-A
To Point-B when excuses possess us,
From bar to bar
Searching, seeking, but never finding
Something
We're told would make a difference,
That would make us stand out
When fully clothed yet vulnerable, nude,
Pierced by the inspector's harsh, objectifying light–

When searching, seeking
To escape the hungry hordes
Like lice.

THE WORD "VISIONARY" IS OVERUSED

Home. Departure. Home. Departure.

Black cat shifts perspective—
The green screen of old-fashioned adventure
Is a dull robe, demeanor, life-mirroring
Darkness—

A writer's life, ho-hum mundanity
Contradicting the veils of supposed
"Experience" phoned into (t)his tale—

(The noun "visionary" is overused)

Feet sitting. Feet standing. Feet leaving.
Feet caught in a never-ending circle.
Feet stagnant as the

Black cat shifts perspective—

The human frame is a chess piece
Beckoned by corporate pawns,
Long-held porcelain,
Malleable, watery forms,
Indelible ideas of beauty,
Faux illusions, quantified ghosts
Which scream that all must be pretty,
Easily accessible to the masses.
Never dark. Never daring.

(The adjective "visionary" is overused)

So, even the most trenchant-in-artistry
Souls stand at the gallows of painting
Flowers, penning stories with happy endings,
Fauxism, excrement hidden under the soil,
Perfumed to give a scent of freshness
To hide its over-processed,
Over-recycled nature.

(The term "visionary" is overused)

It's that which clings inexorably,
Like rotten meat, longings outside of
The work-a-day world, the weekly paycheck,
That cling to the dark musk,
Cling to the tender,
Sweet flesh of the man, woman, individual,
Individuals wearing the aforementioned robe(s),
Writing frantically, stringing together sentences
Like a six-month old just learning to speak
In hopes that the gathered coven,
Critics, potential admirers also dressed
In garbs of black to symbolize conformity,
Old ideals, which cling to the skin like
Rotten trash needing to be taken to the junkyard,
Will proclaim that the work is "Brilliant ", "Striking",
"Original",
"Brand new"—

A frantically-drawn bowl of fruit
Etched in a beginner's art
Class,
A frantically-drawn rose,
A classroom kid starting
His first speech with
"The dictionary defines X as Y",
The million other cliches gnawing at my fingertips,
Whispering in my ear
Every time I, myself, put on the garb,
Adorn myself in the writer's life,
And all the other tired beliefs of excellence
Falling asleep at our feet,
At the ties of our collective robe
'Til they are lied to, told how great they are.

Black cat shifts perspective—

The word "visionary" is overused.

THE GOD IN ME WILL EMERGE

condemned by the madding crowd
    to toil with body raw, whipped,
howling, teeth rattling, loud

chest expanding breathlessly
    as the warehouse/
social/financial obligations, the tree

of life, circles outside the cross,
    provides the dying man
with drink, swallowing heartily

shadows of a mother figure
    cloaks of black, holes
in hands, weeping feet

forced to leave a trail of blood—
    —caked flesh in the sands of judgment
where I leave my body

    to pen my life
in the fleshy rings of forever
    amid the aging woods of self

as I clock in, clock out,
    watch the clock, ponder the clock
and know that in time—

when physicality is past
    and the laughter cast at my artistic failure
is now the hanging, crucified form before all

and the hammering storms of emancipation
    crack the skulls of my self-fulfilling prophecy
to reveal the stony tablets of my divine will—

the god in me will emerge.

I'M BEING CRUCIFIED

My feet slump,
But remain stiff, sturdy, strong,
Upright.
The weight of the world,
My bloodstained cross,
Is fastened tightly to my
Pierced, aching flesh!

I'm being crucified!

Bills, labor,
Manufactured ambitions
Cast into a pre-conceived
Idea of happiness—
A smile, plastic, addressed
To my accusers–

For they know not what they do!

For I know that I, we, humanity
Were meant to do
Better things,
Serve as better vessels
While aboard the seas
Of physicality!
We
Were meant to create, commune.
Yet, all I see, sense, feel
Is mutiny!

I'm being crucified!

And no one hears my cries
As I struggle for movement,
Temporary comfort.

And no one hears my cries
As the nails of time, judgment
Hammer my hands, feet, art into place
And all I get is rejection from publishers,
Peers

Because the visage I craft
Is either "Too normal", "Too weird",
Or "Too in-between".

It doesn't fit into the commonly accepted,
Trendy mold of what is unique.
A notion that is, in itself, generic,
Tired, routine

But thoughtlessly accepted by most!

I'm being crucified!

I try to teach to a crowd of no one
And all I get are jeers, ghosts,
Glares from the robbers, thieves
On both sides of me!

I'm being crucified!

I scream at the god, father, muse
That has forsaken me
In my final breaths

But, no divine form, hope
Manifests
To carry me away!

I'm being crucified!

But, resurrection will come!

I will walk out of the tombs made for me,
Leave these physical constraints
Forcing the wind, the rain,
The masses to follow!

I'm being crucified!

But, resurrection will come

In just a few days, years, lives,
Centuries time!

I'm being crucified!

ALL OF EARTH IS A CHURCH
AND NO ONE WANTS MY RELIGION

All of Earth is a church
        And no one wants my religion.

So, I strut down the aisles, passing pews
        Nervous, confused,
Whitman-like
        Singing songs of self
To a choir of ghosts
        With Medusa-like snakes spilling
From their heads, their mouths;
        A tongue, a leaf,
        A pen, a sheaf
Of paper–
        A razor to a wrist
Permanently scribbling gory bits of insanity
        Hurled at a too-sane world

        Where indoctrinations, generations
Will once find themselves
        Regressing under critical, doctoral observation

        Falling, falling

For the same tune, the same dance
        That has hypnotized humanity,
Put it under their spell,
        A trance
One can interpret as heaven or hell

        Falling, falling

Once more into the purgatory, fire,
        The preacher, I,
Puts out another book, weaves another psalm

        Hoping the congregation
Will hear my divine words,
        Feel my holy, verbal reverberation
Fueling their lips, their electric palms
        Their eclectic, pre-manufactured
Sensations

        Falling, falling

The ghosts, the snakes
        Spill their innards,
        Hisses, chained groans,
        Words against the screeching floor
And with a cold shoulder they leave,
        Predictably ignore,
        My philosophy, my message,
        My mortal qualms

Screaming, "All of Earth is a church.
No one wants your religion anymore."

THE GOD OF EVERYTHING AND NOTHING, THE LANDLORD OF THE DEAD

The vulture then the owl took flight
In synchronicity with the crimson-toothed bite,

The maggot-ridden hordes of Earthly, reanimated flesh
That peeled my skin from bone as a fresh
Burst of liberation, death, formed 'round my core
In the candlelit darkness where a wolfish door

Whispered that life blinded me to the god within
And the undead beast I was to become, now imprisoned,
Was a chance to seek the hidden key, individuality,
Haunting my mind, a specter of immortality,

For the land of the dead I thought I escaped
Was more prevalent here, a madness draped
By the rhythmic pecking of the vulture, owl
At my extremities, their demonic scowl

A mere sign that the gods, goddesses which recline
Here, whispering words, offering me milk, honey, wine,

Are psychological tricks, lies, personifications
Of the beasts lurking, sadistic gesticulations
Of vultures, snakes crawling in and out of graves
Looking for a soul lost, a body to become a slave

To the grind of consumption, the act of seeking
Only to survive. Thus, amid the reeking
Scent of those dead and dying
Did I realize that I was a bridge to both worlds, defying

Sensibilities this will, perceived ability to choose,
Withering with the ravenous mouths foul with hungry ooze,
The ghouls pulling me in out and of existence,
Gods, goddesses killing me in both worlds, in a sense.

At the iron bars of this ethereal cemetery, my gaze spread
Wraith-like, a vision, final thought bled
From the root of the soil, my still leaking head,
That I am the God of Everything and Nothing,
The Landlord of the Dead.

frozen villager
animalistic circle—
earth discovers god

DEAR DIVINE FORMS,
I BEG OF THEE
TO SIMPLY, SINCERELY
TYPE "THE END"

Swinging axe style
Historical deconstruction—
A mortal-minded malfunction—
Masculine, feminine,
Unisex features of the decades:
Gory gashes, knees over glass
Personifying ideals, entire worlds,
Once romanticized thoughts
Lives have been lost over—
Wars with cannons raging,
Eternal crossfire smoldering from rings,
A momentary ceasefire
(Both man and woman carry
The child, victim, in their arms
But only one can be considered
The birth giver, the caregiver etc.) —
Incendiary, "out of context"
Planets unexplored, ignored
For one would rather blindly judge
Than bother to see
Where the fatality,
Uncomfortable history,
Derived, stemmed from,
What went initially wrong
(Thus, continues the war)
Inside the hymn-like song
Of the once "enlightened",
The once professed "intellectual"
Now spitened,
Glossed over as a product
Of his, her, their time
As the clock ticks,
Age-old arguments roar like lions
With the playful echo of kittens

And nothing is learned

And nothing is burned
But all is fuel for the fire

In the fleshy folds of inanity,
In the fields of desire.

WE NEED TO REBEL AS WILDLY, CHAOTICALLY
AS WE POSSIBLY CAN

We need to rebel as wildly, chaotically
As we possibly can—
With internalized frustration stemming
To social progression,
Never outward violence—
To the weariness of the feet
Treading the same path of mildness,
Meekness, shyness, uniformity,
To the stereotypes, presumed abilities
That still cling to some
Based on the characteristics that meet
The eye when one only wants
To skim the surface.

We need to rebel as wildly, chaotically
As we possibly can
By reading the books,
Banned, burned, or otherwise condemned
By society,
Seeing the films, understanding the art
That those in power, those who desperately
Want us to remain a quiet mouse who only
Comes out of his hole in the wall when
He must perform his daily duties
For a collective of higher-ups, reiterating
Pre-established ideas for those who will
Never try to understand the unique,
Life-changing skill, the climate-changing
Stratum you possess in your mighty frame.

We need to rebel as chaotically, wildly
As we possibly can
By consuming, creating art
And, in so doing, healing those with truth
In all its beautiful, broken forms!

We need to rebel as chaotically, wildly
As we possibly can
By speaking with intelligence, eloquence,
Respect, and an always uplifting nature
Towards the downtrodden,
Those who are the repeated victim
Of a fractured system, a society, a psyche
That only wants to see certain individuals
Stuck in a cycle of repeated situations,
Being used, abused by a government
That is only concerned with their own
Benefit once they are given the seat of power,
A mindset that echoes "I am the problem"
While never pointing the finger where it should
Be directed: Towards the authoritative powers
That continue to emphasize, even profit
Off these patterns.

More than anything,
We need to rebel as wildly, chaotically
As we possibly can
With patience, dignity, grace
By repackaging, reshaping
Who we are, the idea of what we can do,
By thinking aloud and by being
Thoughtful at an even greater volume.

We need to rebel as chaotically, wildly
As we possibly can
By giving and accepting love,
By realizing the boxes in which
We are placed at birth
And also, gently, burning them to the ground!

We need to rebel as chaotically, wildly
As we possibly can
For the conquered will soon become
The conqueror.

A TEACHER PREACHING SUMMERTIME IN THE EVER-FRUITFUL GARDEN OF THE SENSIBILITIES

When the phrase "I don't want to be like…"
Ruminates, a psychic with closed eyes,
Inside the gray interior of my corpse blue lips
With a sticky awfulness one can only deem,
For lack of a better word, "nostalgia"—
A bitter taste the mouth is long exhausted
With familiarizing itself with, pressing against,
Black bile held back to momentarily appease,
Black bile held back to simply avoid the
Conflict the villain of our tale so desperately
Craves, goes out of his way to create–

When the phrase presents
The vision of an emotionless facade,
A barrier, a face without character, anger,
Hope being erected to protect
The fragile, onion-layer heart,
The sensitive, empathetic artist's soul
From a father and his narcissistic tirades,
Deliberate attempts to provoke a reaction
Built on highs and lows, a faux need
To meet his impossible standards, satisfaction
Unwanted and unmet
Pierces the arctic glass of the essence
And the hawk, sparrow-filled cerebellum
Echoes a potential conclusion to your sentence
With a solemn "…him",
A mere pronoun but a vulgar, indelible image
That shifts your attitude towards
The kids you are raising into a
Physical, symbolic crossroads

Where one path leads you to think that
Wounding your children by being just like
Your abuser, in a way that completely
Robs of them of their self-esteem for the
Better part of four decades, crushes their ability
To form meaningful friendships,
Makes them socially awkward
And doubtful in all avenues of existence
(Just like he did to me),
Wounding your children in a way that says
That it is okay to fashion yourself after the erroneous
Model of fatherhood
That is now smashed and fallen,
Now exposed for all of its faults, false promises,
Fissures before your feet,
A broken mirror
You were told was your reflection but
You knew within the most intimate chasms of
Your being was not you at all
Through the perfectly imperfect
Microscopic lens of time,
Who doesn't heal all wounds
But, instead, acts more like a specialist nurse
Caring for the long-term patient, I,
By jotting down notes, observations,
Seeds of wisdom which will eventually
Bloom into lifelong lessons in how not to
Act in the ever-fruitful garden of the sensibilities–

And the other path, the one you happily chose,
The one so many do not have the foresight to see as
Even an option (Thus, forever continuing
The combative cycle of father and child), where
You see your adolescent model of fatherhood
As the result of a sickness,

A long undiagnosed mental health
Issue that you can pull away from
Gradually,
Willfully
With great patience, love, and dedication–

A path
Which presents, in its revelatory luminosity,
Your grief as a teacher preaching summertime
In the ever-fruitful garden of the sensibilities.

A LIFE PASSED, A LIFE IN NEED

The palm-sized,
Blue-lined Dixie cup holds life,
Water,
Extinguished—

A tiny,
Slick-to-the-touch corpse

In service of a life,
A daughter's cherished goldfish,

A funeral 'round the toilet bowl
Echoing
A family gathered,
Reiterated words of praise
For the thumb-like creature
Once slithering with red,
Bubbly life

Now immobile as the tears
Spilling sideways,
Sorrow-punctured gasps
From the young mother
Of the aged beast.

And the world stops inward,
The morning outside
As distant, cold, and still as ever

As the school bus the
Family was so desperately
Rushing towards,
Hoping to flag down
By rushing through
Breakfast, the daily routine,
The ever on-coming 9-5
Is forgotten,

A ghost on the road
Who evaporated
Before he arrived,

In service

Of a life
Passed
And a life
In need.

THE BEAUTIFUL PAIN OF A VOW TAKING FLIGHT

The tiny, eager hands of my children,
Which, in their earliest stages,
Held onto my pointer finger as if it were a fist,
As if it were a promise,
A still standing bridge to the past and the present,
As if it were all the good things in and of life itself,
Now cradles glowing phones,
Trophies for memorizing Bible verses,
For placing highly in horse shows,
Along with an arrangement of academic awards,
And as my mind flashes to memories of their younger days,
Their tiny, eager hands digging in the backyard,
Helping my wife work in her garden in the spring,
And, comically, oftentimes
Ignoring a chip to put their whole fist in dip,
I ponder the beautiful pain of an enduring vow taking flight.

LIKE CONCRETE, A STRANGE HABIT FORMED

Like concrete, a strange habit formed
Years ago, which is now an unbreakable mold,
Another groove in the vinyl soundtrack
Of my existence — Lighting candles,
Putting on a film, reading a book,
Writing, even though the exhaustion
Of the day often makes the words that
Come at these times inferior, half-hearted,
And filling a few hours of my night
With the stillness that the day, as lovely
And fulfilling as it is, seems to push away.

A SMILE NIBBLING STILL

Twenty years older than I should be,
I ponder days off, trailer park
Walks with wife, child, thoughts in tow,
Fishing trips where I caught
Nothing but a fire
That sears the heart
With a smile
Nibbling
Still.

A CHILD-LIKE TASTE OF SUN, LIGHT

Decades of scheduling every cent
As if they were sands in the hour
Glass of time summons guilt for
A mere snack, Combos bag,
A Dollar Store buy
On impulse, a
Child-like taste
Of sun,
Light.

THE SUM OF A LIFE: A ONE-SCENE PLAY

FADE IN:

To the start of a fact-based short film,
What should be an unwieldy ten-hour biopic,
Where a tiny bit of cinematic script
Detailing my net worth,
The value of the millions of souls
Just like me,
Hovers gently over the nondescript
Mundanity of my facial features,
Drips down onto my tattered clothing,
Dissipates into my time-tarnished
Rings, watches,
Flesh
(Or lack thereof)
And silently screams,
A trio of skeletons
In black tights dancing
On a gymnastics table,
"Tacky! Poor! Uneducated!"

And the attentive audience,
More "fiscally responsible" souls
Than I,
Casually elucidate their armchair commentary,
The machinery of their minds predicting
The arc, the fate of my character,
Well known to their opulent next door buddies,
Who pompously crowd the theater
With their pinky-upturned boos and hisses
And 90-minute shrieks to the manager
("There's a gummy on my shoe!
Now whatcha gonna do?"),
Filling the theater with their boisterous
Laughter at my plight

Before the divine screenwriter, I,
Can formulate a line of dialogue
More accurate, more fitting
Than the text-like bubble
That seems so close to my mouth
I mine as well be exhaling dollar signs
(Which, come to think of it,
I might've been doing all along,
Which, come to think of it,
I might've been doing
Since the inception of my
Autobiographical song!)

Before the divine screenwriter, I,
Can even make myself relatable
To the spectators razzing,
Mirrors of my own insecurities
Hissing at the snake-like reflection
Coiled,
Set to strike at my twisting,
Upturned mouth
In dollar signs, numeric code,

A bit of expository nonsense,
The same text-like bubble
Dictating my worth
To cinema patrons
Nationally,
Internationally,
'Round the internal globe.

                                    FADE OUT.

A FALSE GLIMMER TO THE NOSTALGIC MIND

Even a workplace I long despised
Hits the nostalgic mind with a
Flash, a false glimmer, longing
To return to this place
If only for a
Day, a shift, a
Walk in feet
Hopeful,
Young.

I, LITERARY EXPLORER, FOUND VOICE, SELF

I miss frequenting the library,
Seeing my autographed books
On the shelf, the hopeful sense
Of summer curling in
On soft toes as I,
Literary
Explorer,
Found voice,
Self.

A MIRRORED PROJECTION

I saw the goddess in you
Long before pearls, palaces fell to your feet!
To merely gaze at you
Is to know the smirk of divinity, to greet
The mortal form of greatness, brilliance, perfection
In a world dim to such sights; a mirrored projection.

LET ME DRINK OF YOUR NECTAR, SWEET SPRING!

Let me drink of your nectar, sweet spring,
And leave the harsh winters outside our door!
Our Earthly strife is fleeting!
In darkness, forever's fruit is ours to explore!
Let us depart from judgment's ever-watchful eye
And descend to our rightful kingdom, you and I!

THE BEAUTIFUL BEASTS BEFORE THEM

Their fate was an elevator to the underworld!
Thus, the couple blossomed in fields of darkness.
Outside of social norms with arms, legs, toes curled
Away from naysayers deeming them "heartless"—
The unruly mortal mob who cannot fathom
Their burden, the beautiful beasts before them!

pounding raindrops–
i hear your apologies
in soft, hollow splats.

THE ONCE IN-DEPTH WORLD OF OUR WORDS

Our conversations have become stale,
Dull pleasantries that defy the
Once in-depth world of our words,
That which lifted us onto
Backs of ecstasy,
As if we're scared
To offend
Our bound
Years.

A GUST (A GHAST):
THE HORROR OF THE FINDING
CREATION IN THE COMMONPLACE

A gust (a ghast)—scribbling to find myself where meaning is translucent, a monotone voice inside a bottle slipping through unfocused hands, down sorrow-stained steps, through the earth, through the core, back into the pink slime of the eye heart where weeping is vulgarity oozing from rules that stain the flesh and fleshy yellow interior by asking to listen to its demands— a cheap date costing forever in nickels thrust down alleys where junkyard fish are stacked in neat rows like display trophies and the only award we receive for our F (erts) is witticism misspelled, mispronounced as a system, shackle, a tool to keep the eyes open and the sun willful, subservient (i.e. mere rays bent).

LIFE, FRESHLY FALLEN

Open, stained glass window
The serpent of my sanity
Fell to life from—

The shadows eclipsed
Slithering tongue sensibilities
As the ghouls breathed winter

-like promises into the ruddy heart
Twisted outside it's summer-like nest–
Soul, graveyard where the zombies

Ate dirt all their lives
And came for a revenge
That starved, left etchings on bones—

More than hunger,
More than the cinema screen,
We hide from life, freshly fallen.

HOWL OF THE CRAZED
EYE FISH SEA MONSTER
BATHING IN OCEANS OF BLOOD

sinewy
extremities reach—
fleshless skeleton walks—

black and white fog–
1930's film monster
lurks with fangs drawn

feverishly scratching,
frantically pawing
shape behind the door—

portal opens
cinema screen
drowns the audience in blood—

past mistakes
ugly mirror image
reaches through glass

moon overtakes sun
silver bullet bursts
permanent paradigm—

innards outwards
weeping red corpse
feasts in silence—

madness glows
from toothy streams—
a monstrous siren—

howl of the crazed
eye fish sea monster
bathing in oceans of blood.

A LIFE TAKES HOLD, OR THE WOLF MAN (2024)

Smooth ocean wave finger sails over
The prickly light red, tall-standing meadows of
Unshaven stubble the 7 a.m. hour again dictates

As an ethereal vision blooms like a hippy child
Sunflower wearing peace sign binoculars amid
The unkempt grasslands, routine personal maintenance,
Of cold-shouldering the mechanical monster
Of this laborious, all-consuming step

And just going about my day

And then another revolutionary wide-eyed daydream
Floods my mental plane
Of wildly abandoning this tired box
On the morning checklist
Forever

And another deliberation pushes
Its liberated extremities through
The slush piles of my gray matter
Of becoming like Lon Chaney, Jr. in
*The Wolf Man (*1941):
Fully bearded, unkempt,
Hair crescenting in rolls against
My scalp and knuckles,
Overgrown claws extended as I
Howl ravenously at the moon
And stalk my prey within the
Claustrophobic exterior setting of the fog-laden woods
In eye-popping black and white
While a loop of ominous instrumentation,
My own personal theme song of dread-infused apprehension,
Adds a classically atmospheric thrust
To the soundtrack.

Then, a more dangerous sensation stirs
The strings of the eager essence

Of renouncing, with a similarly icy ignorance,
The endless hours of societally mandated menial labor,
The endless decades of societally mandated money chasing,
The endless heaps of "must pay" bills,
A societally mandated prison sentence
Cast to every individual for the mere crime
Of living life, occupying space, and breathing breath,
The wintry mountains of every other brand of upkeep
And responsibility we are supposed to travel
With a smile plastered like glue to our
Goofy faces, tongue hanging like a dog sticking
It's head out the window during a blissful, blistering summer drive.

And with the unborn child of these contemplations
Ready to be pushed into existence

A razor whispers

And a life takes hold.

THE POTENTIAL, IMPENDING EMPTINESS (OF THE HEAD)

Serpent slithers from socket to skull.

I fear it all
Being said;
The potential, impending emptiness
Of the head.

My fervent artistry
Wheezing, blue lipped,
Ignored.

For the daylong struggle
Has stretched my bones
To coughing dust–

Hoarse, screaming,
"I don't understand this world!
I don't belong to this world!
I wish I was a song to this world!"

…The Tabby cat
Laps up my milky breakfast…

Another distraction from my purpose–

Growing wild, like my hair!

Growing down (growing up
Is overrated),
Scribbling rhymes from melted
Mental crayons on walls—

A profound
Beat; a heart hiccuping,
Long stalled.

GLASS CORRIDORS

Matching the silver, gray walls,
The dust-laden dying room mirror calls
The white-robed, white-horned
Creature to look, mourn,
Peer from ever-shut eyes,
To acknowledge, actualize
His purgatory, the sin committed
By his lies, his hands around necks fitted,
The grief caused, seas of melancholy cast
In order to die, not relive his past.
Still, his sight remains stagnant, sideways
As glass corridors redirect him through life's maze.

"SUCH IS LIFE," THE SLITHERING CENTURIES WHISPER

Wheels squeak, a wild animal
in winter snow, a gory streak,
the wagon painted red, a thought

as the mustachioed man,
gray hair twirling merrily
around his quivering lips scans

the exterior, horses snort,
the lonely,
claustrophobic landscape transports

his mind to the stars, his true home,
his time machine avalanches
as the aliens, dinosaurs, humans he

amassed, collected throughout the centuries
he traveled, are footprints bearing down on him,
breathing down his neck, a mark, a fear,

a vision of a future world drowning in content
without a raft, without a sense of artistic
appreciation for craft, confident storytelling

swirls in his brain, his senses, a cold chill
summons zombified goosebumps to rise
on dead flesh as he sees a man, a 21st century one

with his face, struggling for words, struggling
to create long after he has said all that he has to say
so he experiments with the same sentiments, content

(there's that word again)

while struggling to stay afloat in a sinking ship of accruing,
increasing expenses, all cast towards luxuries the world
forces the hands, the eye, the heart of the modern mortal

to worship, to believe is worth an entire lifetime of struggle
and he sees romance, fleeting, children growing, budding
between his arms and loss, inevitable, as is the case in all

the centuries he has traveled, but still he returns to the footprints
and thinks of its symbolism of movement, progress, possible
accompaniment as he looks to see the blizzard encasing his feet,

a gasp forming, another thought that this tale should have some type
of moral, lesson, climax, revelation here, but the wind is howling and
snow keeps falling and time keeps boxing him in.

"Such is life," the slithering centuries whisper.

"Such is life," he pens.

THE MOST INTIMATE FORM OF GOSSIP

The most intimate form of gossip:

The mind playing telephone to the heart as the nimble seamstress, the frantic fingertips spill decades of secrets without the bonds of a pausing mouth.

The most intimate form of gossip:

The psyche untangling the culmination of its observations, the hushed details from neighbors and passersby who fill the desolate corridors of our hours, our days with the infinite space of an outside existence coinciding, co-existing, becoming our own via the blue blood, black ink shed from the vulnerable, moving wound of the pulsating pen, the gyrating quill to the milk white, tender bone of the trembling folio… if only for a fleeting photo flash of a moment.

The most intimate form of gossip:

Stopping. Listening. Becoming one with the lover waving goodbye for the last time as she pulls away from her partner in a blur of tears and confused grunts of anger, regret (for we only get one go at all the most beautiful things in life) via the ever-watchful, ever-timeless eye of our literary conceptions.

The most intimate form of gossip:

Hearing the pieces of said lover's heart clatter in an expunged cloud of pipetail smoke, wheel-spinning debris as our heroine exits the scene, the curtain closes on stage left, and the tale, born from both your past and your imagination, concludes with a sense of triumph, dramatic satisfaction.

The most intimate form of gossip:

Forming eternal works of art about your narcissistic father, your generally dysfunctional childhood under the safety blanket of fiction, which covers head to toe in a child-like fort of nostalgia while blocking its associated pain, while joyously interpreting the satisfied cry of accomplishment in doing so as new scars fuse over old generational wounds.

The most intimate form of gossip:

Molding luminous insecurities, contradictions, controlling mechanisms, even a trip to the gas station with your kids into a lighthouse beacon via writing, the most intimate form of gossip, into a signal that will call a cacophony of lonely boats filled with readers who relate homeward: a waving arm of familiarity, comfort in this ocean of a world that is anything but soothing.

Such a glorious merger, a reaction to corporeal events threaded through stacked sheets, lined notebooks, humming laptops reiterates our need as scribes, faithful members enacting the rites of the most intimate form of gossip, to put it all on the page.

For it's these characters and their characteristics, in all their trivialities and revelations, which makes our journey through the motions of learning and aging, that of life itself, and our quest as columnists, correspondents, biographers: to trap all these bits of information, however important or seemingly insignificant, inside the ever-hearing, ever-understanding ear of the unburdened verso and reflect them back to the glass-less mirror of our audience.

The most intimate form of gossip:

Writers, the most intimate gossipers, jotting down love, vengeance, being in all its various forms in the most gleefully unfiltered way.

A WEARY TRAVELER ON THE BYWAYS OF INVENTION

(AN OPEN LETTER TO AI WRITING TOOLS)

Oh, faux Dickens, faux Shakespeare, AI writing tools,

The future is not a machine! An algorithm cannot replace the fathomless depths of profundity which propel the human experience!

Traces of emotion without the thumb and forefinger pinch of knowing them cannot generate the intricacies of the heart, oh, faux King, faux Grisham, AI writing tools, just as your jumbled, electronic charge of cliched storytelling devices cannot replicate the singular journey that is the blood-pumping geysers, veiny stratums, turbulent triumphs of the mortal, fleshy form!

You will never overtake the true thinker, intellect, injector of authorian life, the earthly spirit, oh, faux Joyce, faux Orwell, which so deftly, vividly recalls the sudden jolts, dips, eclipsing peaks, and luminous valleys of our physical, mental wandering! For we, unlike you, oh, faux Blake, faux Milton, can perfectly describe every joyous, agonizing curve on the map of our interior being: a consequence of our own environmental, self programming!

Oh, faux Kafka, faux Hesse, there are no bouts of lingering torment, psychology, involvement behind your electronic mask! Thus, your feeble stabs at composition, as well as those who inject you into the physical frame of their poetry and prose, are similar frauds! Therefore, the curse of the Imposter Syndrome courses through and defines you!

Oh, faux Emerson, faux Whitman, AI writing tools, your whiny, inescapable older brother, Autotune, has poisoned the once righteous, innovative waters of our modern music! Now you wish to pollute the once budding clouds of another form of art mere mortals hold dear, oh, faux Neruda, faux Hughes, AI writing tools, that of the literary world, with the soulless, mechanical serpent of your coiled venoms!

Oh, faux Conan Doyle, faux Chrichton, AI writing tools, your sets of text and code, however numerous, cannot replicate the worlds, verbal galaxies, immortal cosmos of ink we as mortals, members of the earthly spirit, have inside of us! All of which we whispered into existence with the sheer willpower of our fingers, minds, life lessons collectively raging!

Regardless, this artificial takedown by artificial auteurs arrives from a deeply human flaw: wanting something too quickly and with as little effort on our behalf as possible. Still, there is a chance to wipe you out completely, oh, faux Homer, faux Alighieri, AI writing tools. For all we have to do to signal your demise is to ignore and refuse to use you! This will come far easier than anticipated if we have as much patience in our craft as we do the ultimate outcome, monumental quality of our work!

For if a piece is done collaboratively is it wholly our own? Do we deserve to stand in the light of mutual admiration, acclaim, respect from our peers if the colleague is autonomous? Don't we, as a populace, crave that intimate, ceremonious knowledge that a product of our manufacture fully encompasses the indelible imprint, the threads quilting our own distinct essence?

Oh, faux Tolstoy, faux Austen, AI writing tools, for your crimes against the pen, in all its beautiful, illimitable manifestations, may your extinction from the creative plane be fast and imminent!

For the future is not a machine! An algorithm cannot replace the fathomless depths of profundity which propel the human experience!

Sincerely,

A weary traveler on the byways of invention.

THE PAINTING LIED

The painting lied to the child as he passed the timeworn hallway of his grandparents' centuries old planet, Familial Thoughts, Routine Interactions.

The mistlike portrait wordlessly added a note of opulent ease to features that had only known poverty, struggle in their physical form.

The work, woven by an unknown hand, told of a life of sunny valleys. Nonetheless, only serpent-laden mountains of woe had greeted the lady, the boy's great-grandmother, hanging on the wall.

Yet, it told one truth: even the most distorted view of family can summon inspiration. Even hope.

A BRIEF CONTEMPLATION OF A LONG LIFE

Inside the cavernous living room of my darkened mouth, my chipped front tooth and my social anxiety sat down to write their life story.

Thinking of how to begin, they found comfort, as they always did, in silence.

There was a long spell of contemplation.

Suddenly, through hefty typewriter-like clacks via the tip of my tongue, they penned: "It took me forty years to like myself. Maybe in my next lifetime I can learn to love myself."

Heartily nodding, they knew nothing more needed to be said.

CEMETERY MOTHER

Cemetery mother, anguish doesn't define the shears of sanity slipping, clattering from your trembling palms! It doesn't define your aching, dirt-stained knees, the ripped velvet of your sapphire blouse, the heaving, hefty chest sighs with which society brands you in born title, position!

Cemetery mother, life makes us all crawl and dig, often morbidly, just as you must do!

Cemetery mother, we weep, crouched over the cracking tombstones of ancient, newfound woes, just as you must do!

Cemetery mother, life is fleeting: a whisper to all! Thus, breath is sacred!

Some get one. Some get all, cemetery mother!

IN A STOLEN VEHICLE OF INSIGHT

An amorous yarn unfurls
                        Into a luminous ball of kerosene
                        Light,
                        A woefully misbegotten
                        Ideal of mo(u)rning,
                        An overly romantic,
                        Overly romanticized sunset
                        Deliberately combusts,
                        Explodes
                        As the sandal-toed feet of the dinosaur

                        Meets the western gunslinger
At low midnight:
                        The 1950's B-movie monster
                        Sinks her teeth into twenty-something teenagers
                                                    In a daytime
drive-in

A TV set planted amid historic ruins of the cavernous planet, Dystopia,
       Where thoughts remain pointed towards the cinder-laden

                        Eye of the corralled, flame-snorting bull,
                        Invention, but remain
                        The same
                                                  In a
                                        slumped-over stupor
An equine cop forgets to feed his hungry human
                                        In a self-
                                        made stable of
                                        stupidity
                        And everything looks ugly
                        And everything looks beautiful
                        And everything looks bland
                        And forgettable as a rose
                                        In the
gardens of sentimentality

                                                           In the
pitchy, octave-confused
                              Notes that rise
Above the motionless mouths of high-schoolers in love

                              And the birds tweet nonsense
                              From trees of vanity,
                              Which encapsulate, hang,
                              And condemn them
                              To saying everything
                              And, in turn, saying nothing
                                                           In the faux
                                                     musical of
                                                     modernity,
                              Masculinity disguised
                                                           In rocks,
bricks, heavy stones
                              Thoughts the world doesn't
                              Want to feel the weight of
                              So, it points without looking

                                                           In a self-
made stable of stupidity
Above the motionless mouths of nine-year-old adults

                              Who tweet self-centered,
                              Self-aggrandized phrases

About "growing up", "financial responsibility", and other

                              Self-made malarky–
                              Feasts for the turkey
                              Thankful to not have been axed
                                                           In the
slasher film of this love story

      We call mundanity
      Where the frantic, frenetic, hyperbole
      (A hyper bully
               In his own
right)

      Robs banks of syntax

In a stolen vehicle of insight.

A UNIFORM, "ONE SIZE FITS ALL" POPULACE

    effects of the butterfly   with weighted wings split by the
crashing comet   that killed dinosaurs   like me   backwards
  hourglass   time   a Ray Bradbury thunderstruck din   the social media
                     serpent extends a friendly hand
          crotalus horridus swallows venom until I am used up
  a cue to strike   at my throbbing neck   a swig of extreme
                          alcohol
    the carpet rolled   body tossed   in shallow waters
  I (eye) bob for breath
                     apologize, like always,
                           for being   less than
                   you expect me to be
                     a hollow apology
                        to my youngest kin   for
                only making $20 an hour
                     twice the wage of a so-called
                "slave"
                     after 17 years slashing cotton
                in the field
                   a robotic grim reaper
                   with dollar signs in eyes and
                for ear and toe rings
though we are all   indentured   servants
     to the full-bushed, pubic hip sway pseudo sexual   pseudo
intellectual
categories   markets   coffins   we all must
societally fit into

                         a uniform, "one size fits all"
populace
                         bobbing head   for
                the fruit
                of a dream   a better chance
something new
                       before we are something old
           more vulgar imagery
                 (a daisy growing proudly in a
pot

                                        unaware that it is stationary,
trapped
                                        in concrete soil)

                                        of whom we should be
comma for the grammar   with a period in between the word
                                                offense is my only defense
as with everyone
                                        I pettle, paddle towards the
sun
                                        But, my flesh is baked
an oven with wires chewed
                                        (the mailman lovingly yells,
                                        "Hey, idiot, your cookies are
                                done!")

                                        and we should abandon sense
            like clothes
strip consciousness bare
                        and make it play Truth or Dare
                        some dumb kissing game
                                                                It's
the only way to find
                                        the vaginal pearl
pink treasure
                                                of our true self
                                                this infant-like
babbling
                                        I gaga-gooed here
until we drink from the bosom of truth
                                        melting flesh
during the midnight hour
                                        when we, vampires
all,
                                        hunger for this
uncooked meat
                                        The most
and are   most likely
        to try
                                                new things.

(AND I HAVE NO STORY TO TELL AND I HAVE NO STORY TO TELL AND I HAVE NO)

muzzle mouthed red stop sign cardiovascularly whispers blurts
adolescent ghosts tree lined dreams reveries I can only
visit in vaguest moments where freedom can be expelled a familiar Tupac song
(and I have no story to tell and I have no story to tell and I have no story to tell)
as the direction of the literary wind courses backwards and I labor and wait
and I labor and wait and the doctor of medical mediocrity addresses my
self-proclaimed
mental geysers wounds shortcomings capsized waves of creativity
with a band-aid a maggot hanging onto a trash can lid a self-offense from myself cast at snoring audiences a crimson-eyed migraine drown in popping sounds pills, coffee another stale daily routine
the warehouseman, like above mentioned maggot, keeps holding on
after forty years of effort that amounts to feet dangling over a cliff with only the briefest glimpse
of pink valleys steaming burritos notebooks filled with pen slimed, rhythmic jargon
said author calls "poetry"-- ha ha! Alas, what a simpleton!
(and I have no story to tell and I have no story to tell and I have no story to tell)
And I labor and wait and skeleton claw from skeleton crew
screeches, whispers in the bat ear
thy corporeal chest fist to just read more authors, submit to more publishers,
Put more dimpled credits on
the crinkle cut countenance of thy balled up in higher-up laden fist
(and all will be better and all will be better and all will be
?)

                      akin to good
               adjacent to the basement of not too bad
       but, I'm locked down here and I don't think anyone will hear my cries
and my clenched knuckles reverberate   only to my own ears   the stony tablet
      which seeks the ancient wine of the already stone drunk   over diluted
                              senses
           and after half a lifetime I'm still as thirsty as the soil
                   in the winter
       with a perspective as isolated   dis   jointed
        as the dirty dish my daughter hurriedly ate breakfast on
                before school last year
         and left to linger in the back of my new car
                  all summer
(and I have no story to tell   and I have no story to tell and I have no story to tell)

MY VAMPIRE SELF HAS HIS DAY

2 a.m. warehouse lunch, Taco Bell run
The night shift draped over a single-starred canvas
Where lurks yellow-toothed demons of loneliness, a sense of
Wide-eyed slumber, the ever-present question of
"What am I doing with my life?
Where am I going?
Will I ever be my own firmament, bursting bright
In the cosmos of public acclaim?
Do my creative endeavors even matter?"

An ageless, aging me
Looking upwards from the lone night shift picnic bench
Cracked, plain, and in need of a paint job
(Like the man now sitting on it,
Frantically swiping his chin,
Feverishly checking his watch,
Shoveling forked bits of flavorless odds and ends
Into his barely ajar mouth).

An ageless, aging me
Going to the late movie, 9:55 p.m. start,
And wondering why I hunger for bean burritos
As much as butter-stabbed, salt-drowned popcorn
(Maybe it's the explosive kernel splash of innocence,
Youthful pearl of nostalgia these fast food fruits
Bring to the darkening,
Pitch-black soul whose overtaken the
Pin-drop quiet prison block of my ageless, aging mind)

An ageless, aging me
Parking at the same spot
In the same vacant theater lot
My bright crimson vehicle
Has settled its mechanical bones upon
Umpteen times before

As it coughed its final pipe tail bit of
Unfiltered combustible cigar smoke
Before spitting out a raspy, egregious "Eh, I quit!"—

An ageless, aging me
Thinking the same thoughts,
Sighing the same sigh

An ageless, aging me
Bored, but nostalgically thrilled,
At the familiar motions,
The deep midnight memories,
Of what is on the life-mimicking
Cinema screen
(Both literally and symbolically)
As well as off it–
The routine anticipation of
The late-night movie experience,
Fighting the thugs who want
To rob my swampy eyes of their slumber
'Til thy (both literal and symbolic)
End credits crawl–

The instance when
Our momentary entertainments,
Our insights into existence itself
Are forced to conclude,
The curtain is made to shut
And all we have is what we gave
The world in our brief,
Low-budget,
90-minute presentation
Titled *Self*

(Like we are all forced to do through the
Luminous, spring-like crest
Of morning, afternoon hours.
Even on our cheeriest days.)

And though the night personifies
Inklings, notions, all vulture and bat-like,
From which
We'd all wish to see the light shy away

The moments of mirror-like reflection,
Harsh as they are,

Give my teething, whining,
Fussy, infant vampire self his day.

I NOW UNDERSTAND THE DEEPLY ENTRENCHED PHILOSOPHICAL UNDERPINNINGS OF WHY OTHER PEOPLE SHOWING UP AT A MOVIE I AM ATTENDING BOTHERS ME SO MUCH

They shuffle loudly like zombies in a business suit
Into the open-eyed daydream
That has already begun
To thread itself across the patchwork quilt of the iris
Bringing their own light, loudness,
Signposts of the real world
I want so desperately for the flickering images
Spinning their eternal visions,
Webs of wisdom, mesmerizing mosaics
Across the looking glass cinema screen
To help me sneak away from the clutches of
With a trail of popcorn,
A screech of sneakers
Like a fork slowly scraping maddeningly across a plate,
A stench of perfume which suffocates the nostrils,
A voice louder than the film itself,
And, most offensively of all,
They don't even offer an
Impolite, let alone a polite,
"Pardon me".

LIKE KURT COBAIN IN A HIGH SCHOOL GYMNASIUM

The enthralling, energetic
Opening riff of Nirvana's "Smells Like Teen Spirit"
Still summons mirror-like visions of the then eight-year-old me,
As awkward as I am now,
Mouth twisting, spastic like a french kiss
Hair parted neatly to the side, but wanting to grow wild
Like the snakes on Medusa's head,
MTV-style,
Raspy, screaming
Like Kurt Cobain
In a high school gymnasium
With cheerleaders dazedly twirling around him
In slow motion with dim lighting

(*Nevermind* will always be the greatest grunge album of all time)

I want to repackage that singular verve that reverberates within
Every time I hear Cobain,
Put it through the verbal notebook, pencil grinder,
Emulate the offbeat symbolism, storytelling
In a way that attracts repeat listens, study.
In a way that is uniquely my own

I want to turn Small Town, Ohio into the new Seattle,
Turn my popcorn-stained, green Aero hoodie
Into the new version of flannel,
My always clean-shaven face, blue Kangol hat
Into the new version of "rugged"

I want my audience to feel the grime in my voice,
My pain, my words, my song
That isn't present anywhere else on my cowering, cowardly person
And relate, reiterate, mimic my mannerisms

(*Nevermind* will always be the greatest grunge album of all time)

I want to become a sonic creature with razor claws,
As if I was spied raising my middle finger to authority *In Utero*
Like Kurt Cobain
In a high school gymnasium
With cheerleaders dazedly twirling around him
In slow motion with dim lighting

(*Nevermind* will always be the greatest grunge album of all time)

I want to be someone else's someone else
They escape to, dream of becoming
When they hear my lyrics, intro drumming

I want to be the voice of the youth, the oppressed
Like a 90's hip hop track
From Tupac, Ice Cube,
Ice-T, or Public Enemy

I want to smooth it out in a distinctly classy,
Classic, ever-youthful way
(Graying chest hair ever-gleaming)
Like a 90's r&b track
By Mariah Carey,
Boyz II Men, or TLC

Like Kurt Cobain
In a high school gymnasium
With cheerleaders dazedly twirling around him
In slow motion with dim lighting

I want to bring so much
Political, social merit,
Elegance, eloquence,
I don't give a fuckness
To my art,
Grime and beauty intermingling
Like a mouth twisting,
Like a french kiss,
Like the snakes on Medusa's head,

Like Kurt Cobain
In a high school gymnasium
With cheerleaders dazedly twirling around him
In slow motion with dim lighting

That the still socially awkward,
Forty/eight-year-old me
Can be clearly spied
Upon hearing the same notes, words, cords
On repeat for decades
With baggy JNCO jeans, roller skates,
Hair and jewelry swaying down
To my knees

I want to be able to resurrect, through my art,
That feeling of being a seen-it-all nine-year-old
Who is inspired, awestruck
By popular culture

(Like I was watching *Jurassic Park* at the drive-in
For the first time on opening weekend, 1993)

That feeling of freedom, non-conformity,
A timeless artist with a unique viewpoint, voice
That feeling that came with the first spins of
Ready to Die, All Eyes on Me,
Enter the Wu-Tang (36 Chambers), and
The Slim Shady LP.

I want to be a testament to a time,
To singular greatness
Like Kurt Cobain
In a high school gymnasium
With cheerleaders dazedly twirling around him
In slow motion with dim lighting

(*Nevermind* will always be the greatest grunge album of all time)

But, first, I gotta be me.

THE UNUSUALLY TALKATIVE, PROFANITY-LIPPED VERSION OF ME

Mid-90's—
The unusually talkative, profanity-lipped version of me
At 11 years old,
Hides gangsta rap CDs from his parents in books,
Bags, drawers because of the badge of honor,
Signature of "(im)maturity",
Guaranteed mark of a "hoodlum"
The EXPLICIT LYRICS label screams
From cracked, abused
Album cases about the
Rugged, uncompromising contents within—
A signpost that brings all the
Elders who witness such a horror show to raspily, fussily cry-out
"The only reason you like this 'music' is because of the sex and the violence!"

I bite down on my tongue
Upon hearing such defamatory language
'Til it draws blood as the tiny, poetry
Loving monster in my chest wants to pop out, a la Ridley Scott's
1979 masterpiece, *Alien*, and hiss at these thoughtless comments
"No, it's the lyrical focus, honesty,
And the
Social mindedness, ya dufus!"

As the unusually talkative, profanity-lipped version of me
Hurries home from school, cranks up his boombox, and
Boots up *Doom* and *Wolfenstein* on the clunky, overgrown
Box frame of a computer housed in the downstairs of his
Adolescent home
That the awkward, blooming shape,
The unusually talkative,
Profanity-lipped version of me,
Uses to desperately forget the routine
Of soul-draining academics that
Has left its bloody imprint on his
Already overwhelmed, dulled,
Burnt to a cinder core

The years pass,
Blurred and bringing forth
Only updated versions of these sights
As the unusually talkative,
Profanity-lipped version of me

Eventually

Learns to love the seclusion.

THESE HIGH-TECH 1950's B-MOVIE EFFECTS

The black and white U.F.O.,
A paper plate with a string attached to the top of it,
Wows adolescent drive-in patrons as a choppy claymation
Tyrannosaurus Rex fights an awkwardly moving
Triceratops, a brilliant Ray Harryhausen effect that
Took months of patience and heartfelt work,
Causes smiles, giddiness,
Ripples of admiration and waves of intensity,
As the flickering, fleeting image, movie
Changes to a 3-D vision of a man in a gorilla suit,
An extraterrestrial helmet atop his head,
And next, the most majestic sight of all,
A man portraying a giant lizard
With spikes on his back, atomic fire for breath,
Weaves lingering impressions, evokes indelible memories
That, like all the most timely and timeless,
Iconic trappings of pop culture
Will capture the imagination of the
Wide-eyed youth
And their youth
For generations to come–

The excitement of these flickering, fleeting images
Will be spoken of, captured,
Remade, reminisced upon, and recaptured
With smiles, giddiness, ripples if admiration,
And waves of intensity
Memorialized by these once cutting-edge,
Awe-inspiring towers of might,

"Primitive" to some,
But "charming, landmark
Signposts of cinematic progress"
To those who truly know and understand
The history of film–

These glowing, flickering jewels,
Mesmerizing memories–

These high-tech 1950's B-movie effects.

FIRE IN THE CRUMBLING CAVES OF A MELODIC PLANET

Rhapsodic smoke rings,
Fire in the crumbling caves of a melodic planet
More technologically advanced than our own–

The sonic astronaut,
Mouth hovering over his woodwind instrument,
Blows breath outside of the box
Society has confined him to for decades

And the monster, True Art, Invention,
Ravenously storms the countryside
Causing nighttime ghost stories
Whispers of its worth over searing campfires

In the deserts of Earth's heart
Where a war rages over if the breath blown,
The world conceived, the world explored
Is brilliantly disappointing or plain brilliant,
Illuminating

And as moans of anger and ecstasy
Circle ears titillated and unaccustomed
To such daunting treks of exploration

The combat between listeners,
Regardless of opinion on what was conceived,
Is in silent agreement that the rampaging creature
Is worthy of his name.

THE BIRD HAS FALLEN FROM THE SKY

The text ashes have long been seeping through your
Screen frame and now the bird has fallen from the sky
With a silent thud, a stifled yawn,
An arm buzzing jolt from its dead eye,
A curtain of the phone screen undrawn.

Yet, the clones of you are so swift that they take your
Physical formations, bouts of moodiness and unease,
And emulate them so seamlessly
That neither the sky nor the ground has time to lament
The departed social media bird.

But, if we could, would we want a eulogy?
Would we want to remember the way you simultaneously
United and divided us?
Will the replications become better at this opposing duality?
Will the human hum continue idly in its corpus?

All that is known is that the bird fell from the sky.
The reporters gather.
They photograph the twisted neck, bloody feathers.
And all we can do is wonder why,
With our heads strained to detect the upcoming weather,

If this is significant or even newsworthy at all
That this particular bird fell from the sky.

A MERE FLOWER–
THE ENTIRE SPECTRUM OF HUMAN EMOTION

A mere flower–
The entire spectrum of human emotion–
Ardor, exhilaration, and melancholy showers
Senses in serene bursts,
Calming twists in the knotty ocean
Of the roots of our communal essence,
Nature and man,
As we all bloom and wilt but once.
Still, an ethereal presence
Whispers reassuringly that we can
Reach the sun as stem and petals extend–
The sways in the breeze are but the body adjusting
To the way we must conform, pretend–
Like the garden of the spirit after winter's harsh dusting:
We break and we bend
As growth, change are welcomed
In all their beautiful symbols and forms
And obstacles like thundering rain drums
The soil around us in hammering storms
Still we, flora and civilian, the united, similar pair,
Celebrate our setbacks, accomplishments
In wake and in wear:
Signposts of our individuality, development,
Loneliness, cracks, dents–
The sorrows we keep to self,
The sorrows we share–

Our personality radiant, unique, still-standing
In triumphant towers,
In singular notions–

A mere flower–
The entire spectrum of human emotion.

SILENT PEASANT SPIRALING DOWNWARD, NOVEMBER TREE

Frail, bareboned, silent peasant
Spiraling downward,
November tree,
Your season of innocence, life,
Like a sickly, stricken child,
Has been taken from you
(As it will all of us)!

The auburn quilt of your fruit, sustenance,
The yellow pop,
Audible crunch of your multi-hued leaves,
Once extremities pushing,
Gravitating mightily towards the sun,
Has gradually descended
From your scrawny flesh, bark,
Struggling, shaking roots
Where rings of memory clasp at,
Impart the existence of your years
Like a fist raised at the ever-triumphant goddess, The Sun

And now, the folks who are supposed to tend to your needs
Actively plan to do away with your remnants.

Your scattered form
Shredded, expunged
Without fanfare, the proper memoriam
Of the growth, change it once symbolized.

Your scattered form:
Black and white trash bags
To be tossed over the shoulder,
Disintegrated with a disinterested grunt
And a wipe of the brow
From underlings who don't dare understand
The sacrifice you've made
For the changing of the guard, winter,
The stations of your service,

The undeniably human chill
All living, dying forms experience
Studying their painful lessons, youthful bloom.

Oh, frail, bareboned, silent peasant
Spiraling downward,
November tree!

GRETA THE MINEX AND THE UNIVERSAL MAGICIAN

From the arctic ruins of the climactic battle, the soil slaughtering, dictatorial command of winter, the curious, ever-searching, ever-seeking velvet eyes, grasping mahogany hooves of the bounding, fist-sized, Sabre-toothed Minex, Greta, searches the yawning chasm of the dimming heavens for the fiery hat, organic sorcery of the March equinox. From this creaking springboard, a mental monsoon runs with gale force feet through the rain forests of Greta's deductive processes, a thoughtful pounding of the inward drums blares with ever-swaying extremities as Greta, the singular entity, the only member of her near-extinct brood, wonders for the first time if there is a universal magician, a "gerous" in Minex terms, behind the shades of day and night. With this contemplation rushing, panting, and out of breath, in sync with Greta's six frantic trotters, her racing pulse as she pushes proudly through the slick, dew-drowned rows of farm lawn, which stand tall above her like human soldiers in unified, swaying worship to the ever-stretching, luminous cosmic ball, the sun, cloaked in an armor of obscurity before her, for an answer to her celestial question.

With such an awe-inspiring solar object poking out like a glorious clown dressed in half-light and half-darkness from the horizon, the wind gently running its cool fingers through Greta's fur, the winged creatures near her merrily chirping and pecking, the blue bodice of the Earth spreading before her, and the sense of contentment curling throughout her four legs, Greta became aware of several awe-inspiring things at once: the beauty of the moment, her surroundings, and of life itself. Though it didn't answer her pressing, omnipotent musings, these resounding realizations were more than enough to set her tiny, galloping heart to a serene clip-clop, an internal trek through the uncharted caves of curiosity wherein she exited a far wiser, more mature creature: one who knew and fully understood how marvelous, how alluring her singularity, independence is, the majesty of all that fills her gaze, and, most importantly, how her panicky appendages, her peg-like incisors, her long ears, her ever-oscillating nose, her miniscule core are one with it all.

celestial rock glow
gray wolf pack praises nature's feet—
man, too, feels altered.

POEM WHERE I CONTEMPLATE THE END OF THE WORLD

2020 Covid cases increase
As the president tells the sick
Their disease isn't real, a "flu",
To ignore masks, safety
Measures and 4 years
Later man screams
In a store
About
A
Can
Of cat
Food going
Up by five cents
And, just as loudly,
He, red-faced, blares that he
Can't do this another four
Years, seeking annoyed, blank faces for
An agreement, a lesson unlearned.

A PHILOSOPHY OF MEMORY

Among the tuneless rust
The eyeless serpents, insects tire
Of a thousand night skies' dust
Thus, they look to the meadows to inspire
Pyramid-like formations,
Evocations, a celestial whistle
From thousands of years of determination
The UFO is woven from the thistle.
Such is the philosophy of memory:
It only recalls the crimson bloom,
The scab, the hurt,
The sunlit roses in an attic
Where was once the murky, basement gloom.

THE SCREECH ON THE CRANK OF PROGRESS

Soft hammer thunk, crack
Shushing gale force cacophony,
Ocean camel rushes to fishy desert

Sunflowers pop red-eyed
Like blisters, explosive mists
Ooze with the neck-like droop

Of the garden nature, man trods
As the celestial cerebrum whistles
Chalkboard nails through cracked teeth

And the white gown matrimony
Of human and nature unkind
Loses its ring at the bent knee proposal

The communion of soil turning to brick
Brick returning to shards, glass
Around which bare feet, souls dance

And feel nothing, but love is spoken
And sung about and given a crumpled rose
From the unholy offspring of said coupling

And pretty pictures are made to eat this glass
Around which bare feet, souls dance
And uncertainty becomes commonplace, certainly

As bulldozers are brought into the framework
And the filmmaker behind it all puffs dank
Nicotine clouds while forcing sense upon the scene

With words of admiration defying his actions:
The crunch of leaves underfoot,
The nickel scented splat

Of the cosmos' head
For which the galaxy mourns
But we, stone-faced, go on pretending

The screech on the crank of progress
Doesn't hurt our own.

THE TALE CLIMAXES IN AN UNEXPECTEDLY OPTIMISTIC WAY

Count the victories,
Few as they are–

Few paths are fully
Entrenched in misery.

Ambition is not dust,
But a star.

ABOUT THE AUTHOR

Andrew Buckner is a multi award-winning filmmaker and screenwriter. His short dark comedy/horror script *Dead Air!* won Best Original Screenwriter at the fourth edition of The Hitchcock Awards.

A noted poet, critic, author, actor, and experimental musician, Buckner runs and writes for the review site AWordofDreams.com.

The God in Me Will Emerge

Andrew Buckner

www.ingramcontent.com/pod-product-compliance
Lightning Source LLC
Chambersburg PA
CBHW060843050426
42453CB00008B/811